Copyright © 2017 Francesca Zampollo
All rights reserved

onlineschooloffooddesign.org

To those who love food
To those who make food
To those who think about food

May this book broaden your creative potentials

THINK
like a
food
designer

60 activities to develop your Food Design Thinking mindset

Francesca Zampollo Ph.D.

		page
1	take the reversal test	18
2	overcome the antropocentrism bias	20
3	overcome the expectation bias	22
4	alternative narrative (1)	26
5	alternative narrative (2)	30
6	alternative narrative (3)	34
7	alternative narrative (4)	38
8	develop empathy for the younger	46
9	develop empathy for the older	50
10	develop empathy for the different	54
11	consider a mango	58
12	consider bottled water	64
13	change the world of food	66
14	change society	68
15	change the natural world	70

		page
(16)	change the world	72
(17)	improve your skills	76
(18)	challenge your ambitions	84
(19)	observe food and relationships	86
(20)	set yourself up for failure. kind of...	90
(21)	learn to be a member of the group	94
(22)	learn to communicate with sketches (1)	96
(23)	learn to communicate with sketches (2)	100
(24)	learn to communicate with sketches (3)	104
(25)	learn to communicate with sketches (4)	108
(26)	learn to visually summarise information (1)	112
(27)	learn to visually summarise information (2)	118
(28)	learn to visually summarise information (3)	122
(29)	learn to learn	128
(30)	spread your search (1)	136

		page
(31)	spread your search (2)	140
(32)	think about needs	144
(33)	unveil the memories behind food	150
(34)	what is your favourite TV food Show?	158
(35)	creativity that solves problems	162
(36)	forced combinations (1)	166
(37)	forced combinations (2)	170
(38)	forced combinations (3)	174
(39)	focus on opportunities	178
(40)	develop metaphorical thinking	180
(41)	what if?	184
(42)	be an explorer	188
(43)	biomimicry inspiration	192
(44)	free your inner weirdo (1)	198
(45)	free your inner weirdo (2)	204

		page
46	reverse your viewpoint	207
47	get accustomed to random associations	210
48	step away from your screen	214
49	wonder	216
50	enjoy solitude	218
51	write a fan letter	220
52	specifically select random words	222
53	take it apart to make it better	224
54	substitute	230
55	combine	234
56	be inspired by others	240
57	make it simple	242
58	senses isolation	246
59	reuse reuse reuse	250
60	what's next for this waste?	254

introduction

A few years ago I was contacted by a client who wanted to implement the Food Design Thinking process into their business. They understood that this methodology, since it combines knowledge of food with a food-specific Design process, would help them achieve higher company goals. So the company put together a group of people who, from that moment, would have become the Food Design team and who would have led all future Food Design projects. I provided the team with a Food Design Thinking process tailored to their needs and accompanied them on their creative journey. Nonetheless, the process wasn't leading to the expected leaps in food innovation. The team members had the resources, but the individuals lacked passion and confidence.

A friend of mine is a baker. He loves his bakery and the history within it, as well as the bread-making process itself. He loves the physical contact with the dough and all the handling, kneading, moving, cutting, and shaping of bread. He loves providing what, at least in Italy, is considered a staple component of every family's table. He has always been interested in experimenting and trying to come up with new shapes of bread or entirely new concepts. One day he spoke to me about how frustrated he was about the fact that every new item he had proposed never really took off. My baker friend had lots of passion but lacked the resources to achieve successful innovation.

These two stories probably summarize everybody's story, one way or the other. Food Design is a fascinating discipline, but success is elusive. If you ask me, the two biggest elements of success within Food Design are people's *attitude* and *aptitude*. In other words, passion and the right resources and skills. My clients had a Food Design Thinking process, but the individuals on the team didn't have the right aptitude and lacked passion for the project. They aren't to blame; nobody is born with a food designer's mindset, and not everybody is always completely in love with the tasks they are assigned. My friend the baker, on the other hand, had the right attitude and exuded passion but did not have the resources and the know-how to generate successful ideas.

...you're here because you love what you do, and you are interested in learning more...

If you are reading this book, something tells me you are passionate about Food Design, and you either want to make Food Design your career or Food Design already is your chosen career and you want to become even better at it.

Either way, you're here because you love what you do, you are interested in learning more, and you're excited about the prospect of generating ideas around food and eating. Since you are here, you already have the right attitude for Food Design Thinking. And that's great because that is something I cannot teach you. Passion, interest, and excitement for Food Design come from within, and nobody can give that to you. All you need now is a little direction and guidance to improve your aptitude, to learn the "how to", and that's exactly why I've written this book, to train you to think like a food designer.

...I will challenge you to think in new ways. I will push you out of your comfort zone...

This book is a collection of 60 exercises that will develop your Food Design Thinking mindset. Through the next two months, with one exercise a day, I will challenge you to think in new ways, I will push you out of your comfort zone, and by doing so, I will teach you to think like a food designer. These exercises will help you develop the right mindset to take on board any Food Design challenge you'll ever face in the future. If you have already experienced a creative process, you might know that the techniques used seem at times challenging and a bit weird. They are usually designed to be playful and to push your thinking towards unknown places because that's exactly what creativity likes, and that is where it flourishes. Not everybody is immediately at ease with the type of elasticity that these processes require. And that's really okay. Most of us are at least a little uncomfortable or dubious with what is new. I have written this book and developed the exercises within it to ease this transition, to help you develop the exact mindset that you will need to practice food creativity. Whether you're a seasoned designer or a complete beginner whose experience with Food Design revolves around a Pinterest board, this book is for you. Whether you want to become a professional food designer or simply want to create memorable dinner parties for your friends, this book will help you get there, by training your creative mind.

I have written this book to help you develop the exact mindset that you will need to practice food creativity

If you are new to Food Design and Food Design Thinking and are unsure if this is for you, don't fear. If you love food, eating, and thinking about food, it's likely that Food Design is indeed for you. **Food Design is the discipline that includes any type of innovation in the field of food and eating**: from cutlery to dishes, from food services like cafes and restaurants to food events, from cakes to bread, from seeds to whole food systems. If Food Design is the "what", then Food Design Thinking is the "how". Food Design Thinking is the answer to the question: How do I design food or anything related to it? **Food Design Thinking is the creative process that takes you from zero to a food concept, passing through investigation of your interests, definition of a design challenge, ideation of a plethora of ideas, and selection of the best one**.

In order to start using Food Design Thinking or any type of

creative process you want to use, the right mindset and a certain elasticity in your way of thinking and approaching problems will help you immensely. This book is a guide to prepare you for any type of food creativity you'll want to explore.

When I was working with the client I mentioned above, and with others before that, I could see what the problem was, but there was little I could do at the time. Team members were a little disinterested, which was coupled with inexperience. It is easy to become frustrated when you first start experiencing a completely new way of doing things, like a creative process, for example. When starting a Food Design Thinking process, you're not really eased into it, you just start. You start doing the activities and using the methods that will spark your creativity, like StarChat, IdeaHive, IdeaMarket, IdeaShake (which I created, and which you can find on Amazon), or some of the most traditional methods like observations, interviews, role plays, brainstorming, SCAMPER, to mention a few. For some people these techniques and methods immediately flow easily, but most of us are not so quick at learning to brake our assumptions, being at ease with the unknown, deflecting biases, communicating visually, and feeling free to be weird. Most of us, I think, benefit from a little mind training to develop these skills and feel completely confident when starting our creative journey in Food Design. And that's why this book now exists. I wanted to give an-

This book is a guide to prepare you for any type of food creativity you'll want to explore

ybody interested in food creativity the possibility to train their creative thinking instead of simply being expected to "get it" immediately.

So, if you own or work in a restaurant, a food company, or design firm interested in using Food Design Thinking, or if you are, or want to become, a baker, a food truck owner, an event planner, or simply the best food entertainer among your friends, dive into this book, give yourself to it, trust the exercises, invest your time and energy in it, and I promise you will develop a creative mindset that will prepare you for any creative food challenge you'll ever face.

Ready?

Let's start…

1

take the reversal test

choose an action that you want to do but you know you shouldn't...

Cognitive scientists came up with the "reversal test" to intervene in loss aversion and negativity bias. Choose an action that you want to do but you know you shouldn't - for example, eating a candy bar that you know is unhealthy for you - and try flipping the script: Instead of saying to yourself, "I won't eat that because it's unhealthy," say to yourself instead, "I just gained $2." Your brain then reallocates the neurochemicals as a reward instead of a loss.

...and try flipping the script

2

overcome the antropocentrism bias

The anthropocentrism or human-centrism bias implies that humans are the most important species of this planet. For example, when you read phrases like "...research on human AND animal studies," you understand that the writer implied that humans are not animals (which they really are...) and furthermore that animals are not considered of equal importance to humans. But, what if they are? What if humans are as important as other animals, as plants, as water or soil? This might seem radical to some, but think about it; if all humans considered themselves of equal importance to any other element on the planet, maybe we would behave differently, operate differently, create differently, design differently, and maybe the world would be just a little bit better.

Choose one animal you usually eat, or whose milk or eggs you eat, and put yourself in its metaphorical shoes. Think of yourself as living a day in its life.

What do you like?

What would you change?

How do you feel?

3

overcome the expectation bias

Take one topic within Food Design and research it until you find at least three unexpected pieces of information.

topic of research

The expectation bias implies that experimenters believe more in their findings when they align with the expectations they have of the outcome, and disbelieve or discard their findings when they conflict with those expectations. In Food Design Thinking in particular, we want not only to include and never discard the findings that are different from our expectations, but we also want to pursue especially those findings. We should always search for what surprises us. If we are not surprised, it means that what we found is what we already assumed, and that's boring. We should challenge our assumptions and expectations and seek the unexpected because there lays excitement and inspiration!

Take one topic within Food Design (any topic that has anything to do with food or eating, e.g. apples, 1750s French recipes, relationship between lights and flavors, synesthesia, insects, Michelin chef's morning routine, whatever you want…) and research it until you find at least three unexpected pieces of information.

Since you have them now, why waste them? Try and come up with one idea (for a product, dish, service, event, or whatever you prefer) that incorporates all three interesting pieces of information.

Congratulations, you are designing =).

unexpected information

my Food Design idea

4

alternative narrative

activity 1

Collect three or four examples of food products, foodservices, or food businesses that offer an alternative narrative to food waste.

According to the United Nations Environment Programme and the World Resources Institute, one-third of all food is wasted worldwide.

The United Nations Environment Programme website states that, "In the United States 30% of all food, worth US$48.3 billion (€32.5 billion), is thrown away each year. It is estimated that about half of the water used to produce this food also goes to waste since agriculture is the largest human use of water. […] 1.4 billion hectares of land - 28% percent of the world's agricultural area - is used annually to produce food that is lost or wasted."

In the United States, an estimated six billion pounds of produce is wasted each year because of its appearance.

In urban areas, fruit and nut trees often go unharvested because people either don't realize that the fruit is edible or they fear that it is contaminated, despite research that shows that urban fruit is usually safe to consume.

What examples can you find of products and companies that are changing this narrative and influencing people to make more sustainable choices?

a story of food aste prevention

a story of upcycling

a story of food waste repurposing

a story of recycling

activity 2

Collect three or four examples of food products, food services, or food businesses that offer an alternative narrative to the excessive and worryingly sugar consumption amongst children and adults.

The recommendation for adults is to not consume more than 25 grams of sugar a day, and yet the average American consumes 82 grams of sugar per day.

With as much as 42 grams of added sugar, one can of soda contains almost double the amount of daily sugar allowance.

Added sugar contains no essential nutrients and is bad for your teeth. Excessive and regular amounts of sugar can cause type II diabetes, cancer, and obesity.

Sugar causes chemical changes in the brain and addiction.

What examples can you find of products and companies that are changing this narrative and influencing people to make healthier choices?

the story of a product

the story of service

a story for children

a story for adults

alternative narrative

activity 3

Collect three or four examples of food products, food services, or food businesses that offer an alternative narrative to "made in…" somewhere far, far away.

In the United Kingdom, for example, 95% of fruit comes from abroad, half of the vegetables are imported, and 30% of all goods transported by lorry around the UK are foodstuffs.

The UK, for example, produces 19 million tons of CO_2 transporting food, 10 million of which is emitted in the UK. Since 1992, the amount of food flown by plane has risen by 140%.

According to freight transport–related projections by the California Air Resources Board, in the USA approximately 950 cases of asthma, 16,870 missed schools days, 43 hospital admissions, and 37 premature deaths could be attributed to the worsened air quality from food imports.

Food miles are not the number-one cause of pollution on this planet (actually agriculture is... still food-related... surprise!), but maybe we can agree that being able to buy avocados in Lapland in January is not a big necessity. Because of how consumerism and markets work, today everything is available to us every day, but as consumers we should stop and think for a moment about what we really need and the impact of our choices. And what can we do as food designers?

What examples can you find of products and companies that are changing this narrative and influencing people to "buy better, buy less, and buy local"?

the story of a product

the story of service

the story of a person

the story of a nation

7

alternative narrative

activity 4

Collect three or four examples of food products, food services, or food businesses that offer an alternative narrative to unethical food production.

The production of palm oil, a major ingredient in many margarines, is causing the extinction of the Asian orangutan.

The cultivation of soya is making the Amazonian rainforest disappear at a rate of five football pitches per minute.

Companies like Tesco and Dole are accused of violating internationally agreed labor standards.

Pink Lady apples (a hybrid of Golden Delicious and Lady Williams) are the first patented apples, so now anyone wanting to plant Pink Lady trees has to pay for this privilege; critics describe this as "bio-piracy", the privatization of our planet's biodiversity.

In India Coca-Cola, the world's largest beverage company, has unlawfully pumped 1.5 million liters of water a day from local reserves, leaving farmers unable to irrigate their crops and draining the community's drinking water supply.

For decades Nestlé has been aggressively marketing its formula to some of the most vulnerable communities in the world, violating the 1981 World Health Organization's International Code of Marketing of Breast Milk Substitutes which prohibits advertisement that may idealize formula and give the impression that it is safer and more nutritious than breast milk.

Today, farmed animals consume 80% of the antibiotics sold in the U.S. Et cetera, et cetera, et cetera.

Even if this is just a glimpse into the unethical standard of food production, we should not feel discouraged. There are, in fact, many, many companies led by caring, intelligent, empathetic people who daily design and work for the production of sustainable food. Go out there, find them, be inspired, and share your findings to inspire others too.

a story of people

a story of animals

a story of innovators

a story of business

what I have learnt from thinking about alternative narratives (activities 1-4)

what I take away and will apply in the future

ETHICS IS NOTHING ELSE THAN REVERENCE FOR LIFE.

Albert Schweitzer

8

develop empathy for the younger

Develop the empathetic ability to understand the motivations, actions, and desires of someone 10, 20, or 30 years younger than you.

Develop an empathetic ability to understand the motivations, actions, and desires of all humans, especially those outside your own lens of understanding. In Food Design Thinking, especially in the first phase of the process, when we expand our horizon and search for information, our biggest goal is empathy.

Imagine having to design a snack, for example, for one specific tribe living in the Amazon. This is a tribe who has never had contact with people outside their own tribe. Imagine designing a product without meeting anyone from this tribe, without talking to them, without visiting where they live and understanding how they live. What do you think you would be able to design? This is an extreme example, but it shows you that we cannot design anything without understanding our users. Designing something that we think our users will understand, use, and like does not mean designing something they will, in fact, understand, use, and like.

It is in this process of understanding the group of people for whom we are designing that we aim for empathy. Only when we have gathered enough information, spoken to enough people, and observed enough environments, as to be able to think what they think, and feel what they feel, only then will we be able to design for them. Empathy is thinking what others think and feeling what others feel.

Develop the empathetic ability to understand the motivations, actions, and desires of someone 10, 20, or 30 years younger than you. If you have a child, or a nephew or a grandson, try and spend time with them, observing them and asking them questions so you can understand the world from their perspective. Narrow the exercise by investigating how they feel about vegetables, for example.

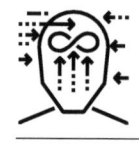

what they value

what they search

what they need

what they feel

9
develop empathy for the older

Develop the empathetic ability to understand the motivations, actions, and desires of someone 30, 40, or 50 years older than you.

If you are so lucky as to have in your life an elderly parent or grandparent (depending on how old you are), try and spend time with them to understand what they think and how they feel about 3D food printing, for example. Ask questions and observe them in various appropriate scenarios until you have collected enough information for you to have developed empathy towards elderlies regarding their views, preferences, and feelings. Do you feel you would be able to design for them now?

what they value

what they search

what they need

what they feel

10
develop empathy with the different

Develop the empathetic ability to understand the motivations, actions, and desires of someone with a different nationality or cultural background.

How do people from a different background view certain topics? What are the differences and similarities with the way you understand and perceive a certain topic? Often we think we know what other people think and feel, but assumptions are a food designer's worst enemy. Grow out of the habit of making assumptions and instead always challenge what you think to be true and seek information that surprises you. Narrow down this specific exercise to what people from a nationality or cultural background different from yours think about meat and fish consumption, for example.

what they value

what they search

what they need

what they feel

11
consider a mango

Consider the social, economic, and environmental impacts of buying mangos at the supermarket (regardless of where you live).

Go to the supermarket, buy a mango, take it home, eat it, and then ask yourself: Where did that mango come from? How did it come here? Who brought it here? Who grew it? What was the salary and working environment of those who grew it? What does mango mean to people in my country? When and how is it eaten? Are there differences between this and when and how mangos are eaten in the country where it is produced? What happens to the peel and seed? Where do they go? How are they processed? For each of the aspects of a mango's life, try and describe the social, economic, and environmental impact.

What have you learnt? What could/should be done differently? Where could a food designer intervene and bring improvement?

Where did that mango come from?

How did it come here?

Who grew it?

What was the salary and working environment of those who grew it?

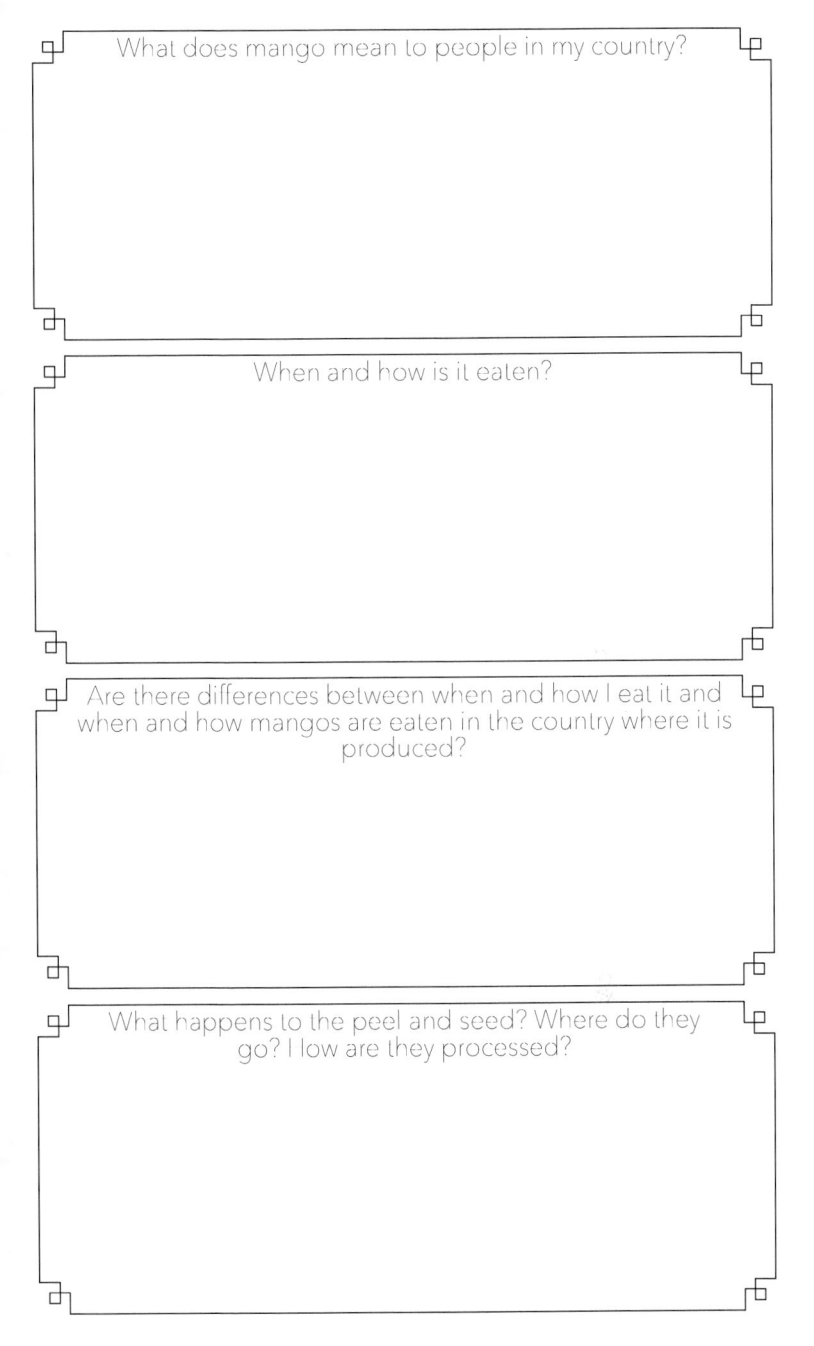

> What does mango mean to people in my country?

> When and how is it eaten?

> Are there differences between when and how I eat it and when and how mangos are eaten in the country where it is produced?

> What happens to the peel and seed? Where do they go? How are they processed?

What have I learnt?

What could/should be done differently?

Where could I intervene and bring improvement?

12

consider bottled water

Consider the social, economic, and environmental impacts of buying bottled water.

Go to the supermarket, convenience store, cafe, or wherever, look at all the different bottled water brands available, take a picture, and do not buy one. Then as soon as you have an Internet connection, open YouTube and watch the video "The Story of Bottled Water" from the YouTube channel *storyofstuffproject*. Now... think.

As food designers, as makers of "new stuff", and ultimately as human beings, we have the responsibility of making good and not bad, of improving and not hindering, of developing and not halting. The damage previous designers and food designers have done is already unbearable. It's now time to take a mandatory action towards a better future, for future generations, for the plants and animals with whom we share Earth, and for Earth itself.

13

change the world of food

Think of what type of food designer you want to be and choose your path. You can always change it or adjust it, but it's going to be of great help to you if you have a clear idea of what you'd like to achieve in life.

What do you want to change in the world of food and eating?

How do you want to make the world a better place through Food Design?

14

change society

What do you want to change in society?

How do you want to improve our society through Food Design?

15

change the natural world

What do you want to change for plants and animals?

How do you want to improve the natural world through Food Design?

16

change the world

Make the decision to actively use Food Design to create the type of change you want to see in the world. What will you do?

What do you want to change in this world?

How do you want to improve the world through Food Design?

WHEN THE WHOLE WORLD IS SILENT, EVEN ONE VOICE BECOMES POWERFUL.

Malala Yousafzai

17

improve your skills

Choose one dish and cook it at least 10 times.

my dish is...

Challenge yourself to constantly improve. Whether you are a seasoned chef, somebody who never held a pan in his life, or anything in between, choose one recipe, make it once a day, and observe yourself improving. It doesn't matter if cooking is not the type of Food Design you are interested in; this is an exercise for you to practice the feeling of improving, to see yourself improve, and learn about how you improve and learn. Whatever is your level of cooking skills, you can always do better. That's being a human being. What is important is for you to accept that wherever you start from, there's always a way to be better. Every day write what you have done that really worked and what you could improve the next time. As a food designer, you should grow that type of humility, which will serve you really well in the initial phase of the Food Design Thinking process when it's time to search for information and learn everything you can about your design challenge. As a side effect of this exercise, you'll end up having at least 10 meals, one better than the other, which you can enjoy in contemplative solitude or in the company of friends and family.

day 1

day 2

day 3

day 4

day 5

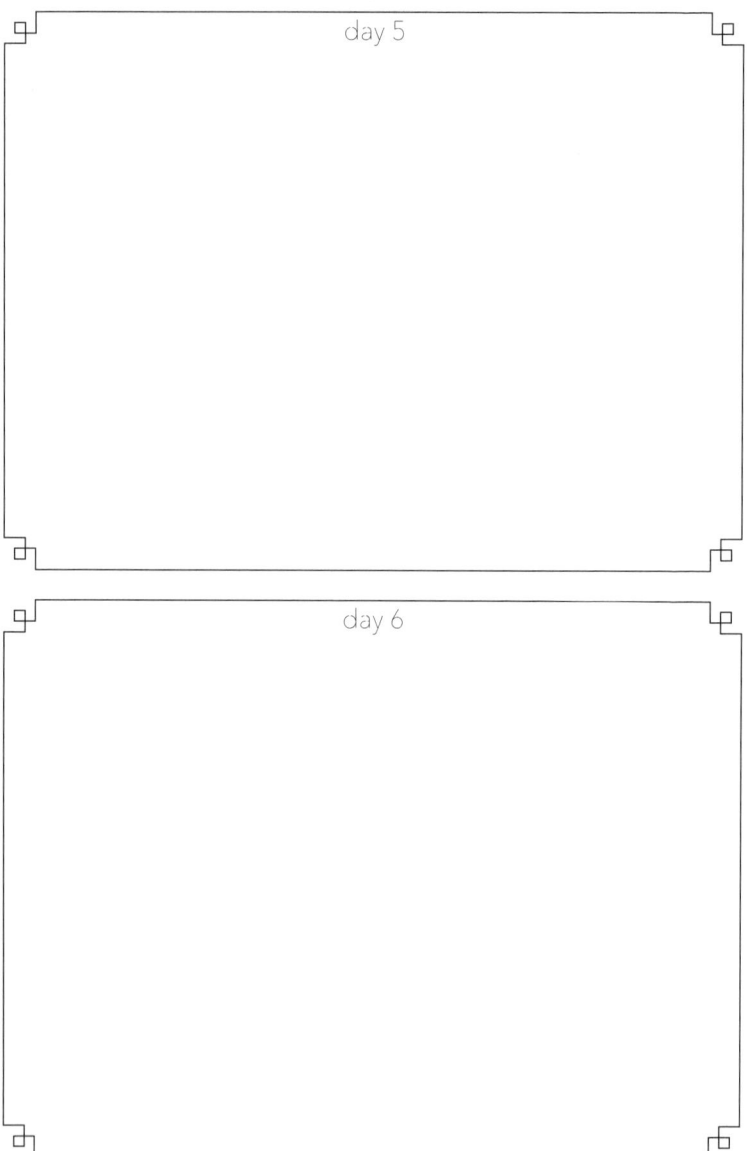

day 6

day 7

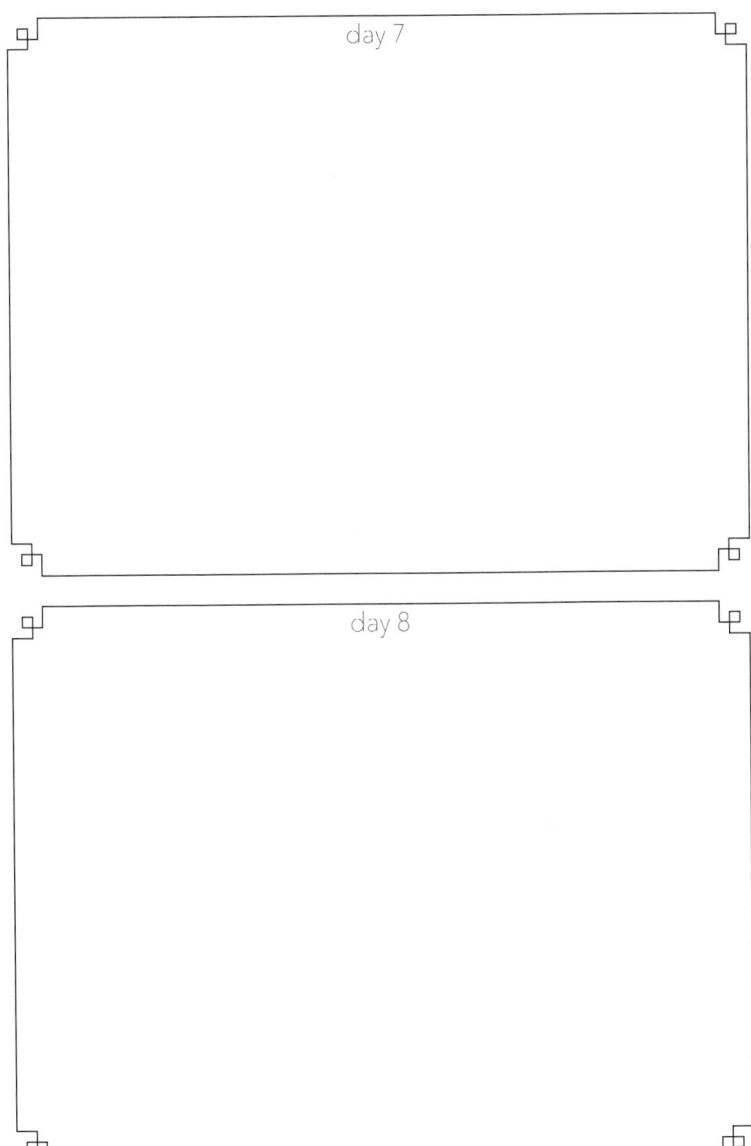

day 8

day 9

day 10

What have I learnt from this activity? What will I apply to my future work?

18
challenge your ambitions

If you were to design anything, literally anything, what would you design? Within your Food Design journey you will probably - almost definitely - find yourself having to choose one option over another: one design challenge over another, one target user over another, or one design idea to develop over another. But how do you choose? There is one trick to always make the right choice: pick ideas and projects that resonate with you but that also challenge you.

If you were to design anything,
what would you design?

19
observe food and relationships

Observe your relationships with other people and learn about the role food has in each one.

Learn about the strong relationship between food and community. Human beings are social animals. We thrive when we are in groups, and we need to have relationships with other human beings. Most of us have multiple types of relationships. We have friends, siblings, parents, and grandparents. We have other family members. We have a romantic partner, co-workers, and people with whom we share a passion (our chess club, dance class members, choir members, etc.). I bet that for you, too, food is somehow, at some point, present in any of these types of relationship. Observe your relationships with other people and learn about the role food has in each one. Conduct observations and ask questions to those around you to really understand, from their perspective, too, the role of food in your relationship.

This exercise, if conducted thoroughly, will generate a considerable amount of valuable insights that you will be able to apply in any Food Design project you'll work on in the future.

RELATIONSHIPS >

When do you eat food together?

Where do you eat food together?

What type of food do you eat?

Why do you eat together, cook together, or eat out together?

What does food do to this relationship?

20
set yourself up for failure. kind of...

That sounds wrong, doesn't it? We're definitely supposed to always set ourselves up for success! But for the scope of this exercise, embrace failure as a strength builder and learn to never be afraid of it. Failure is a part of Food Design. It happens. We all spend time and resources in propositions that don't go far beyond our imagination. And that's okay. Not only is that okay, it is actually necessary. By failing, not only do we learn about ourselves as food designers, but we also, and most importantly, learn about our project and where it should go. Failure is such an integral part of Food Design Thinking, for example, that we put ourselves in the position of failing constantly, and in doing so, never really fail. For example, when we generate ideas for a new product or dish or service, we set out to generate hundreds of ideas. For every 100 design ideas, maybe one or two will get to the end of the process. Does this mean that we failed 98 times? Of course not! I prefer to think about it as having given ourselves 98 more chances to succeed. In this mindset, it is important to learn to fail, to learn to let go, but always learning from what we've had to let go.

So: find at least one thing you're terrible at, do it, observe yourself, and try and understand how you could improve. You should choose one thing that you know you do not do well or that you really don't like doing. Making an omelette? Folding sheets? Recycling? Giving instructions? Chopping vegetables? Whatever it is. Do it a few times and try and figure out what it is that you don't like specifically or that you're not good at. Be specific. You don't necessarily have to impose to yourself to improve - unless you want to - because nobody is good at everything, and that's okay. The most important thing is for you to accept your "failures", learn about them, and figure out how to move past them. Mastering this self-awareness and the ability to accept that not everything that comes out of our mouths (or Food Design Thinking processes) is pure gold makes us better prepared to move forward in our creative process and gives us the serenity of making mistakes. And this is exactly what sets us up for success.

> Find at least one thing you're terrible at, do it, observe yourself, and try and understand how you could improve.

one thing I'm bad at / I don't like doing

details on what I don't do well / correctly / precisely

where I could improve

how I could improve

21
learn to be a member of the group

In Food Design Thinking we work in groups because more people bring in more resources and skills, and a variety of skills and resources (along with a variety of information and ideas) is a key aspect of this methodology. When working in groups, we want to participate and let others participate, without prejudice, without dismissal, and without overpowering the group dynamics with our point of view. It is important to develop the skills necessary to let others shine because you never know what wonders hide inside each member of the group. So, to train you to let go of control, I would like you to take something you think you are very good at doing - making an omelette, folding sheets, pruning a basil plant, washing dishes, decorating a cake, whatever it is - and have someone else do it while you watch them, and without giving any suggestions or directions! Will it feel like torture? Or will it feel liberating?

Take something you think you are very good at doing...

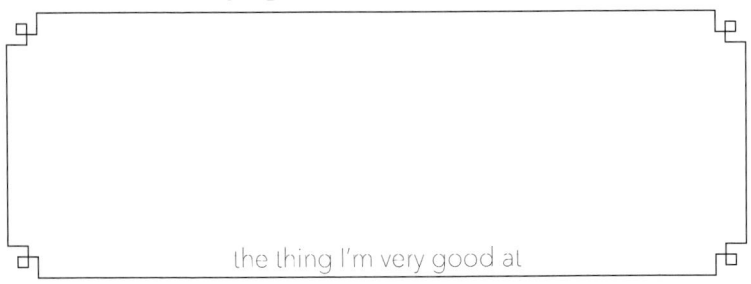

the thing I'm very good at

... and have someone else do it while you watch them, and without giving any suggestions or directions!

how it feels to watch others do it

22

learn to communicate with sketches

activity 1

Sketch a market vegetable stall.

This and other similar exercises in this book do not aim at transforming you into Leonardo Da Vinci. That is not the goal. That is also not necessary. In Food Design Thinking we do sketch and use visual thinking and visual communication - a lot - but this doesn't make Food Design Thinking exclusive to those who are very good at drawing. Believe me, most of us draw stick figures. All you need is to communicate what you see in your mind well enough so that other people see it too. Most of the time sketches have the objective of showing proportions, dimensions, spaces, etc. In addition, one great asset is annotations; they make any plain sketch a great resource. Sketch the shape, make it as understandable as you can, and even so, you will always need to add little arrows with notes specifying the material, the color, the dimensions, etc.

Sketching is supposed to be quick; in the idea generation phase there's really no time to spend on details, so practice making sketches of objects or systems quickly.

Use one or two colors tops, no need for more. Use a pen or marker; don't use a pencil or anything you can erase. What happens if you mess it up? Nothing... Develop confidence. You will notice that sketching is a way of seeing and a way of thinking. You will find yourself realizing things, understanding, and ideating, just through visual representation.

Pro tip: sketching objects is great, but what is really useful is to sketch how they are used.

name of vegetable stall ....
location ....
products sold ....
producer location ....
sketch:

What can I learn?

What works?

What could be improved?

23

learn to communicate with sketches

activity 2

Sketch a restaurant layout
and how people move around it.

Choose a restaurant or eating establishment where you have been a few times and sketch the layout first, and then customers' movements (between entrance, table, toilet, bar, etc.), as well as staff's movements (between reception, kitchen, tables, backstage, till, etc.).

name of restaurant ....
location ....
type of restaurant ....
number of staff members ....
max. number of customers ....
sketch:

What can I learn?

What works?

What could be improved?

24

learn to communicate with sketches

activity 3

Sketch
a dish.

Choose a dish you know well, and sketch first how you've always eaten it, and then create multiple sketches with variations of components' positions, dimensions, colors, and maybe ingredients.

name of dish ....
designer / chef ....
type of dish ....
number of components ....
type of vessel ....
sketch:

What can I learn?

What works?

What could be improved?

25

learn to communicate with sketches

activity 4

Sketch a food truck.

Choose a food truck (or ice cream truck) that you have seen and maybe even eaten at. Sketch how it looks from afar. Sketch the floor plan and its interiors. Sketch details of the interiors: appliances and their positions, flow of movements, etc. Sketch from the point of view of customers and from the point of view of staff and cooks.

name of food truck ....
location ....
type of food ....
number of staff ....
type of food vessels ....
sketch:

What can I learn?

What works?

What could be improved?

26

learn to visually summarize information

activity 1

Visualize with a mind map
how a restaurant works

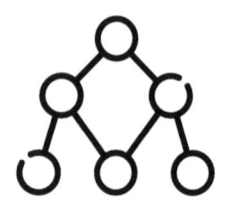

As food designers we communicate visually all the time. Mind maps, in particular, are our best friends. Maps are wonderful for three reasons: They are a fast way of summarizing complex information; they allow us to visualize not only insights but also the relations between them; and they are a great way to communicate that information to other people in our design team. In Food Design Thinking we use them to summarize the insights emerging from our research, and we use them to visualize our ideas. The most important thing to remember is that maps are made of two elements: insights and links. Do not underestimate the importance of links; they are very important because they show connections. It is when you place a link between two insights that you apply critical thinking to your findings and ideas. There are different types of maps, so make sure to experience them all, in this and the other similar exercises. Visualize with a mind map how a restaurant works. Remember to include every aspect of a restaurant, from a customer's point of view, and the restaurateur's point of view.

A **circle map** is used to define the context of a certain topic. A **bubble map** is used to describe the qualities of a certain subject. A **double bubble map** can be used to compare and contrast the qualities of a certain subject.

circle map

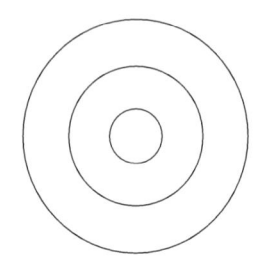

bubble map

double bubble map

A **tree map** is used to hierarchically classify features or elements. A **relationships map** is used to show relationships of features or elements, where links can connect any element. A **flow map** is used to show sequencing and cause and effect.

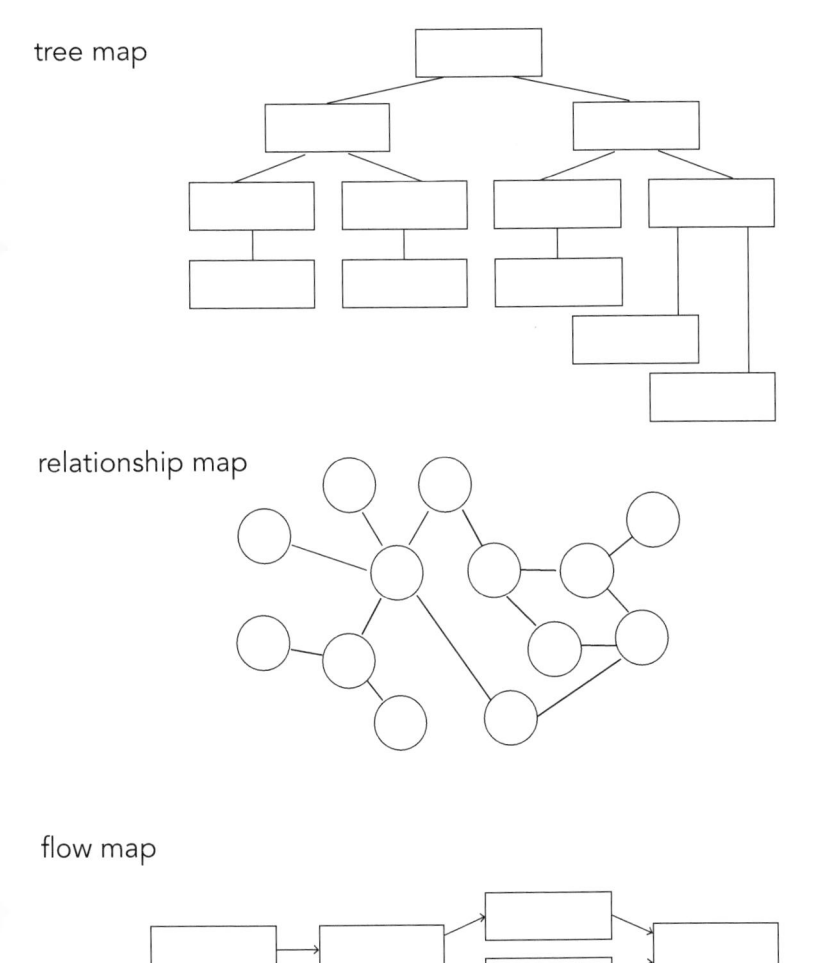

tree map

relationship map

flow map

visual map of how a restaurant works:

27

learn to visually summarize information

activity 2

Visualize with a mind map how a sandwich is made

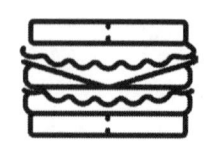

Visualize with a mind map how a sandwich is made. Seems simple? I guarantee that the more you write down elements and their relationships, the more new elements will come to mind. Here you have different ways to approach this mind map. You could, for example, sketch the different components of a sandwich and visualize how these are prepared and put together. You could also visualize where each component comes from, who produced it and how, and how they got to the person making the actual sandwich. You could take the perspective of cultural preferences, energy consumption, culinary adventure, etc. In general, the more you research the topic of sandwiches and sandwich making, the more you learn about it and the more information you can collocate in your map. The more detailed the map, the more detailed your understanding of sandwiches. Researching a certain topic and visualizing what you learn is a key step in Food Design Thinking.

visual map of a sandwich:

28

learn to visually summarize information

activity 3

A simple exercise and another opportunity for you to sharpen your research and visualization skills.

> Visualize with a mind map everything you know and can find out about bananas.

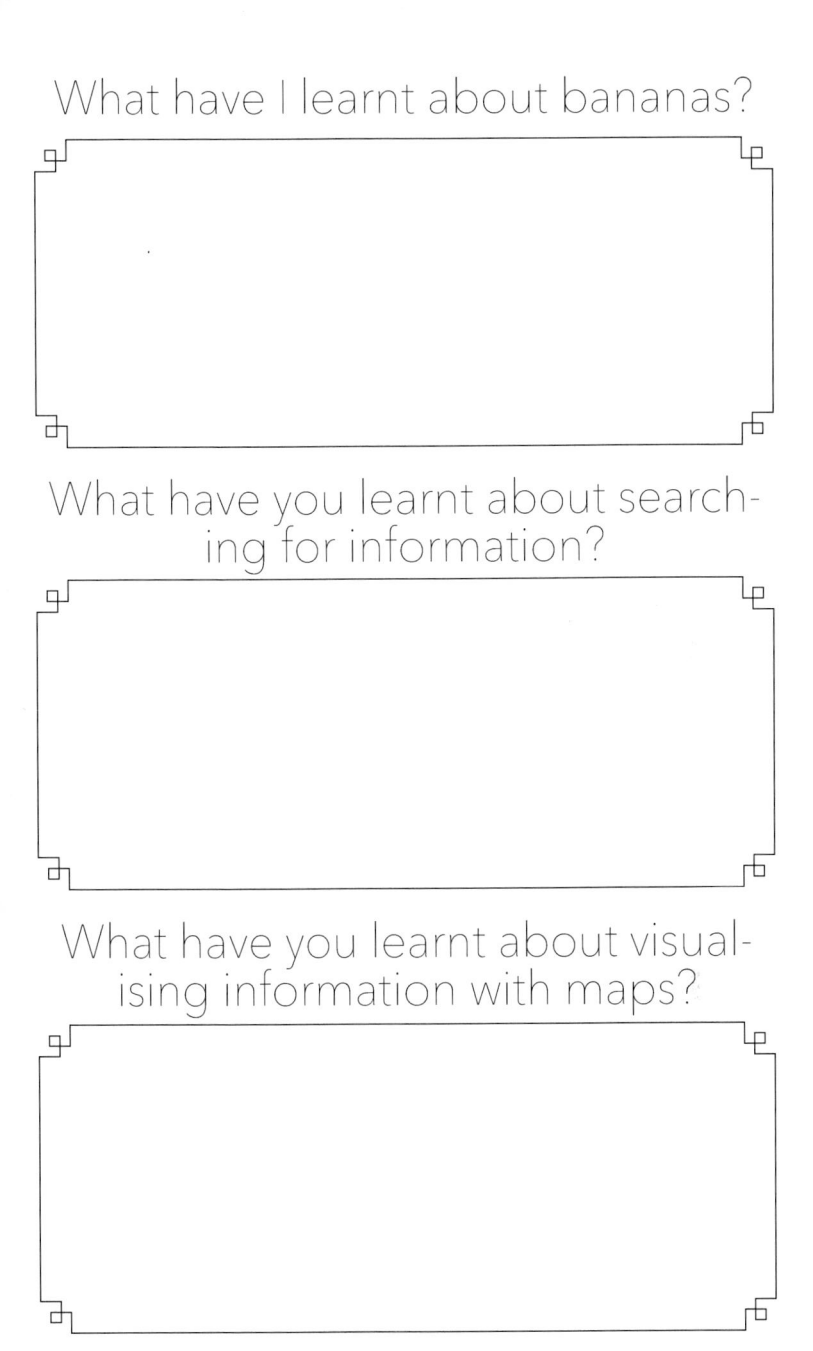

What have I learnt about bananas?

What have you learnt about searching for information?

What have you learnt about visualising information with maps?

visual map of bananas:

YOU CAN'T DO SKETCHES ENOUGH. SKETCH EVERYTHING AND KEEP YOUR CURIOSITY FRESH.

John Singer Sargent

29
learn to learn

For the next seven days, I would like you to learn something new about yourself every day. Start by making a list of everything you already know about yourself. Since this list might be quite long… let's narrow it down to how you relate to others. Once this list is made, then start observing yourself in social situations, and ask questions to those around you, if you need. How do you relate to others in various social situations? Think about how you listen, ask questions, contribute to the conversation. Think about your body language, facial expressions, tone of voice, etc. Apply this self-analysis to different situations like birthday parties, work meetings, family dinners, etc. What are your best characteristics? What could you improve? The knowledge that will emerge from this exercise will help you become a better food designer, and by showing you how to learn about yourself, it will teach you how to learn about others. Learning about our users is a fundamental step in any food project.

> Every day learn something new about how you relate to others.

What I know now about how I relate to others

daily observations

day 1

day 2

day 3

day 4

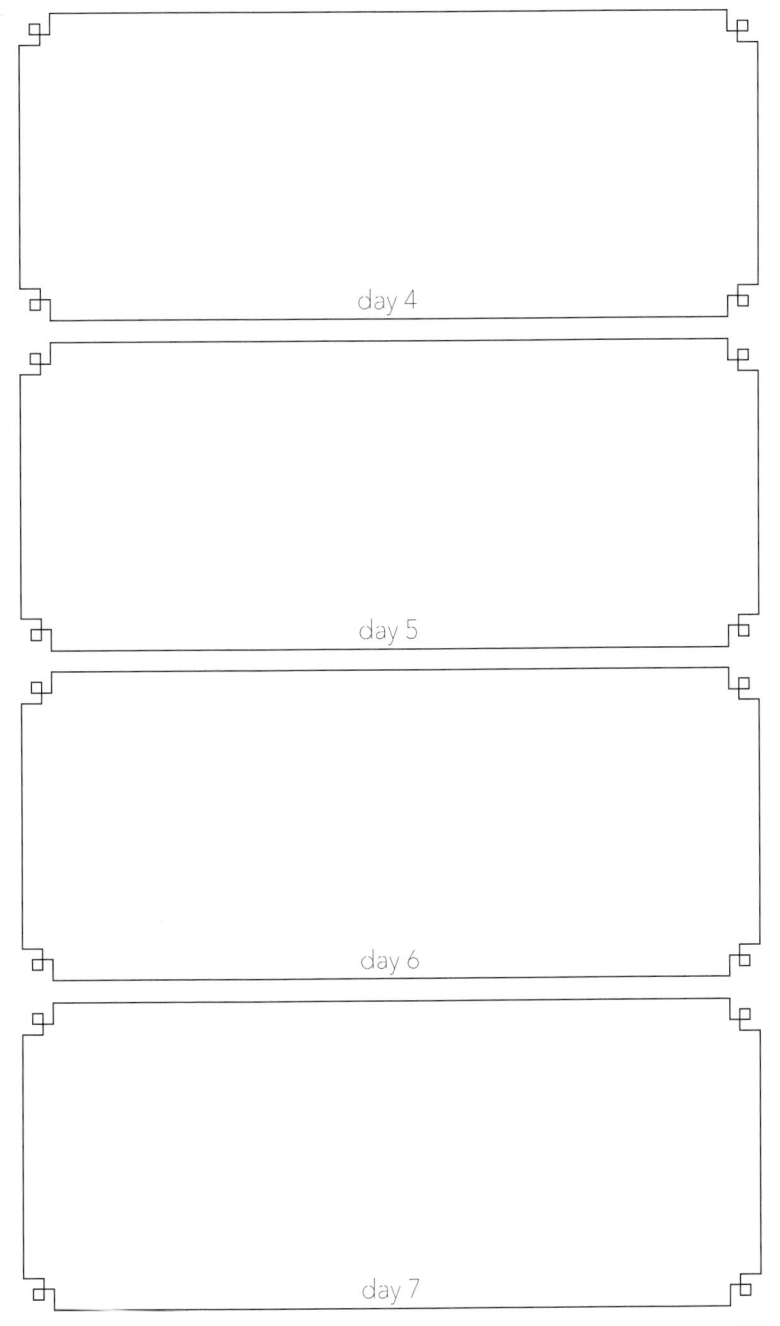

day 5

day 6

day 7

summary of new discoveries

how I listen

how I ask questions

how I contribute to the conversation

my body language

my facial expressions

my tone of voice

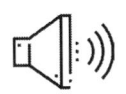

what are my chracteristics?

what could I improve?

30
spread your search
activity 1

Find as many different types of fresh pasta as you can.

I challenge you to find as many different types of fresh pasta as you can. For the scope of this exercise let's define pasta as made of fresh dough with two main ingredients: flour and water. Variations of ingredients of the dough itself are okay (with or without eggs, for example), but we are not interested in the sauce or condiment. Geographic location can vary, but it should not be made for mass production.

With this exercise you learn to never stop with those things you can list on the top of your head, but you learn about the importance of really researching a certain topic. You will be amazed by the number of different pastas that you'll find! And if your list is shorter than 10 items… go back out there!

In addition, searches like these are wonderful opportunities for any food lover to become even more knowledgable with food itself! Think about how, after this exercise, you'll be able to entertain your friends and colleagues with anecdotes about fresh pasta - for example - from all over the world! =)

1.
2.
3.
4.
5.
6.
7.
8.
9.
10.
11.
12.
13.
14.

	15
	16
	17
	18
	19
	20
	21
	22
	23
	24
	25
	26
	27
	28

31

spread your search

activity 2

Find as many types of tomatoes as possible.

I challenge you to find as many types of tomatoes as possible. Hint: There are a lot! Here we enter the world of seeds and biodiversity, something we food designers should be sensitive about.

The way consumerism, mass production, and industrial agriculture has evolved has, unfortunately, brought us to regularly eat only a few types of tomatoes, often regardless of our geographical location. The same thing happened for potatoes, corn, and much more. In your research you will find that there are instead a few companies that aim at finding, growing, and spreading as many varieties as possible of tomatoes, and other vegetables and fruit.

Dive into the beauty of this planet and the variety of what it provides; if you can, stay away from the feeling of sorrow and disappointment for how human beings manipulated this planet and instead take inspiration for designing a better food future.

1.
2.
3.
4.
5.
6.
7.
8.
9.
10.
11.
12.
13.
14.

15
16
17
18
19
20
21
22
23
24
25
26
27
28

32
think about needs

Ask yourself:
do I really need this?

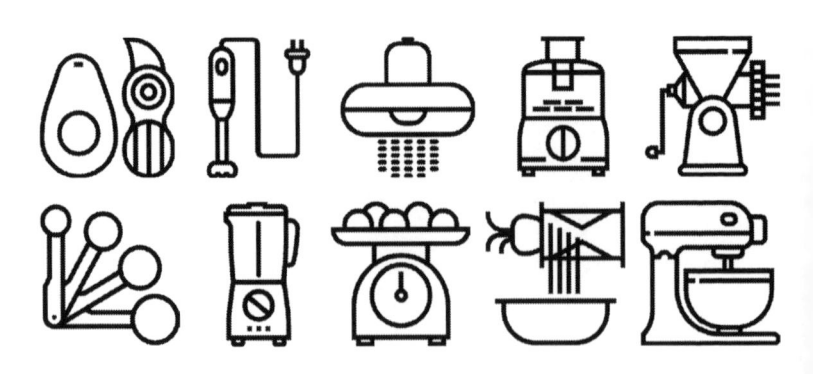

Wherever you are in this moment, look around you. How many man-made things do you see? If you're like most of us, the answer is: countless. The world is filled with stuff. And who filled it? Designers. For decades designers have had the habit of creating problems and providing the solutions. Then marketing told us we can't live without it.

When you are at home, go in your kitchen and try and think of how many of the things you see you use regularly, and how many you haven't used in more than a week, a month, or more. Now reflect on the fact that everything becomes rubbish. Every man-made thing, at some point (a few hours, a few days, months, years, or centuries) is no longer needed or usable, and it becomes rubbish. This rubbish needs to be dealt with somehow: thrown somewhere where we don't see it, burned, and rarely - yes, rarely - recycled. Each of these options takes a lot of energy and resources.

While you stand in your kitchen, opening cupboards and drawers, counting, reflecting, and asking yourself, "Do I really need this?" I would like you take the opportunity for considering what type of food designer you want to become.

Do you want to create problems? Or do you want to solve problems?

stuff I could live without

stuff I use rarely

stuff I use every day

WHAT YOU DO MAKES A DIFFERENCE, AND YOU HAVE TO DECIDE WHAT KIND OF DIFFERENCE YOU WANT TO MAKE.

Jane Goodall

33

unveil the memories behind food

Make a list of the best food memories you have.

It's list-making time! Make a list of the best food memories you have, the food of that memory, who shared that moment with you, and the reason why that moment became embedded in your memory. Then ask 10 other people about their best food memories. What do you learn about food? What makes food memorable? How will you use these insights in your future Food Design projects?

my memorable food

food	shared with

why is it so memorable?

friends and family's memorable food

food | shared with

why is it so memorable?

What do you learn about food?

What makes food memorable?

How will you use these insights in your future Food Design projects?

34

what is you favorite TV food show?

Binge watch as many TV food shows as possible with the goal of learning something new.

Food is everywhere on TV, which gives us food designers a wonderful way to learn about our favorite subjects: food and eating. So, I would like to challenge you to binge watch as many TV food shows as possible with the goal of learning something new. Watch cooking shows where professionals or amateurs cook, food documentaries, and whatever other food-related program you can find on TV. Is this nothing new to you? Maybe...

For this exercise I would like you to always have this book on your hands and write down anything new you can learn about food and eating. Don't forget to broaden your spectrum. Consider cultural, social, and environmental perspectives.

Then make a mind map of your insights (every surprising new thing you have learnt). If your map fits into a regular A4 printing sheet, then you haven't spent enough time watching TV! =) Learn more. And now, how will you use these insights in your future Food Design projects?

	cooking shows	food/eating shows
name of show		
insights		

documentaries			other		

make a map of your insights

35

creativity that solves problems

What if tomorrow your kitchen and all kitchens on the planet disappeared? You wake up and puff… vanished. You can buy your food, but there are no cooking appliances, no knives, no plates and pots, no ovens, nothing…

Design one recipe that doesn't need any cooking appliances or cooking utensils to be prepared.

my recipe

CREATIVITY TAKES COURAGE

Henri Matisse

36

forced combinations

activity 1

Design a dish or a food product that conceptually combines Japanese ramen and Mexican tacos.

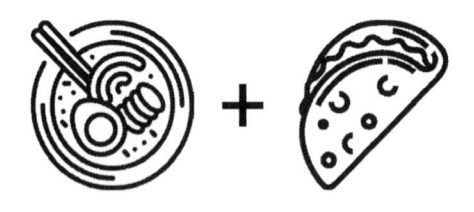

Creativity often sparks when combining two unrelated ideas, concepts, or items; so design a dish or a food product that conceptually combines Japanese ramen and Mexican tacos.

Is your brain telling you, "This is ridiculous," and "Don't be foolish"? If it is, just acknowledge that and... ignore it!

Our brain is trained to simplify in order to allow us to be efficient. This is also detrimental to creativity, so while it is okay to simplify in many other aspects of our lives, it is not a good idea at all to follow that advice in food creativity. The Food Design Thinking methodology is designed for you to let your creativity shine, and creativity likes challenges. So... challenge yourself with this forced combination, and have fun!

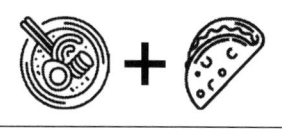

37

forced combinations

activity 2

Design a dish, a food product, or a food service that conceptually combines "wilderness" and "laughter".

You can think of anything, as long as the final idea combines - somehow - the concept, or elements of, wilderness, and laughter. Sounds weird? Well, it's supposed to be! In the Food Design Thinking ideation phase, you will find yourself juggling similar tasks, so this is your opportunity to train yourself to tackle them.

Remember, creativity often sparks when connecting distant and unrelated ideas. Moreover, creativity likes a fun and playful atmosphere. Hence... becoming accostomed to weird situations, and tasks!

38

forced combinations

activity 3

Design a dish, a food product, or a food service that conceptually combines "potatoes" and the "Pythagorean theorem".

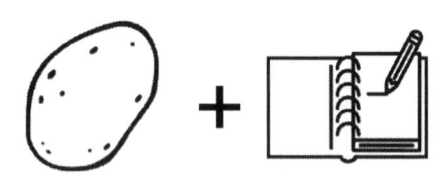

What on earth! Right? I know… But creativity likes challenges, even if often our brain doesn't. So, sit down (or walk around, whatever works best for you), and think of how you can combine these two very distant concepts into an edible product or an entire food service.

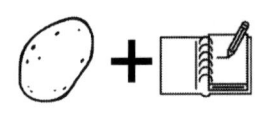

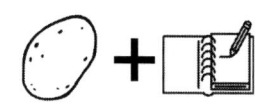

focus on opportunities

Do not focus on problems; focus on opportunities.

In the design world, for years the trend has been about solving problems. So much so that very often - too often - designers created problems that they could then solve. Luckily nowadays, in Food Design as well, we are shifting from problems to opportunities. Working on opportunities rather than problems is like opening a door into infinite possibilities instead of opening a tiny box containing only one.

How to phrase an opportunity: First of all, the focus should be on the opportunity gap, not the product/dish/service that will fill it. Secondly, I personally like phrasing opportunities as questions because I think questions sound like opening new spaces and leave room to discovery. Here is an example. Problem: *Design an indoor plant-growing kit*. Likely solution: an indoor plant-growing kit. Opportunity: *How can we enable people to grow their own plants, learn about seeds, and the importance of biodiversity?* Possible solutions: Seeds delivery service, biodiversity and plant-growing workshops, seed and instruction booklet attached to supermarket salad bags, etc…

List at least three Food Design opportunities you would like to work on.

40
develop metaphorical thinking

Make a metaphor for a project you're currently working on.

Metaphors are a great tool to transform complex ideas into something easier to understand. They are a way to give meaning to what is new and unknown. Metaphors are, in fact, the way we learn. We understand the unfamiliar by means of the similarities it has with what is familiar. Metaphors are also quite useful in helping us get a different perspective on a problem. Make a metaphor for a project you're currently working on (or an opportunity you want to investigate). Simply compare your project or opportunity to something else and then list the similarities between these two. What you are doing is using one idea to highlight another. See how many similarities you can find!

Examples:

Designing a way to transport doughnuts is like pruning a tree.

My life is like a room full of open doors.

Finding the best restaurant in town is like putting out a fire.

Remember, metaphors need to make sense to you; don't worry about others. What is important is for you to list the similarities between your project and its metaphor. Here is where the metaphor will provide you with new perspectives and insights.

TIP: I. A. Richards describes the two parts of a metaphor as being the tenor and the vehicle. The tenor is the subject to which attributes are ascribed (your project or opportunity in this case), and the vehicle is the object whose attributes are borrowed.

my metaphor:

(tenor: your project/opportunity)

is like

(vehicle)

similarities between
tenor and vehicle:

vehicle's characteristics that you
want to apply to your project:

(41) what if?

Since human beings have the ability to symbolize experiences, our thinking is not limited to the tangible and to what is happening now. Abstract thinking, in fact, allows us to imagine and anticipate the future and generate ideas that do not correspond to what we have already experienced. This is one of human beings' biggest asset and certainly food designers' greatest tool. One of the ways to exercise abstract thinking is to ask and answer "what if" questions, which is also a fun way to train your food designer's mindset.

Simply ask "what if…" and complete the question with a contrary-to-fact condition, idea, or situation. Then answer that question with a train of thoughts made of answers and backup questions. Never just answer with a few words, but try and really explore that scenario. You can do this asking any type of question, or you can ask "what if" questions that relate to your specific project, by transforming one aspect of your project into a contrary-to-fact condition. Do this exercise often! Also, between you and me, it's a great conversation starter at dinner parties!

Ask and answer "what if" questions.

Start with these:

What if all cows and goats and sheep and camels had a meeting and decided to never again produce milk for humans?

What if our mouth was on the back of our head?

What if humans could communicate with plants?

What if everybody grew their own veggies at home?

What if plants could walk and go where they want?

What if all food in the world was free?

"what if" question

answer

"what if" question

answer

"what if" question

answer

"what if" question

answer

42

be an explorer

To be an explorer you must believe that there is a lot to be explored and discovered. If you go to a museum, you'll find ideas there. If you go to a restaurant, you'll find ideas there. If you go to an amusement park, you'll find ideas there. If you go to the dentist, you'll find ideas there. If you go to the hardware store, you'll find ideas there. Indeed, the more your sources are spread wide, the more original your ideas will be.

> Go out there and search for new ideas or inspirations.

wilderness

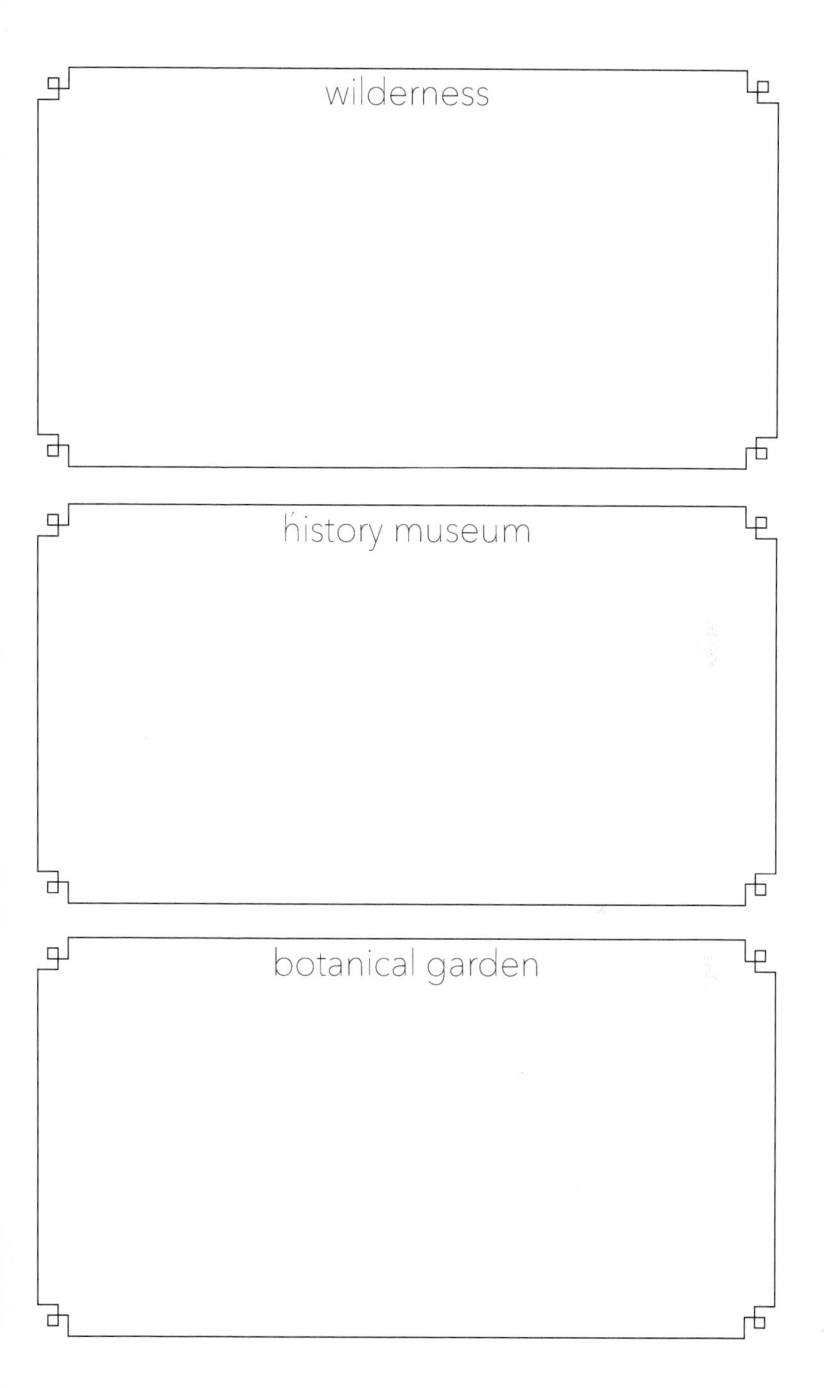

history museum

botanical garden

second-hand shop

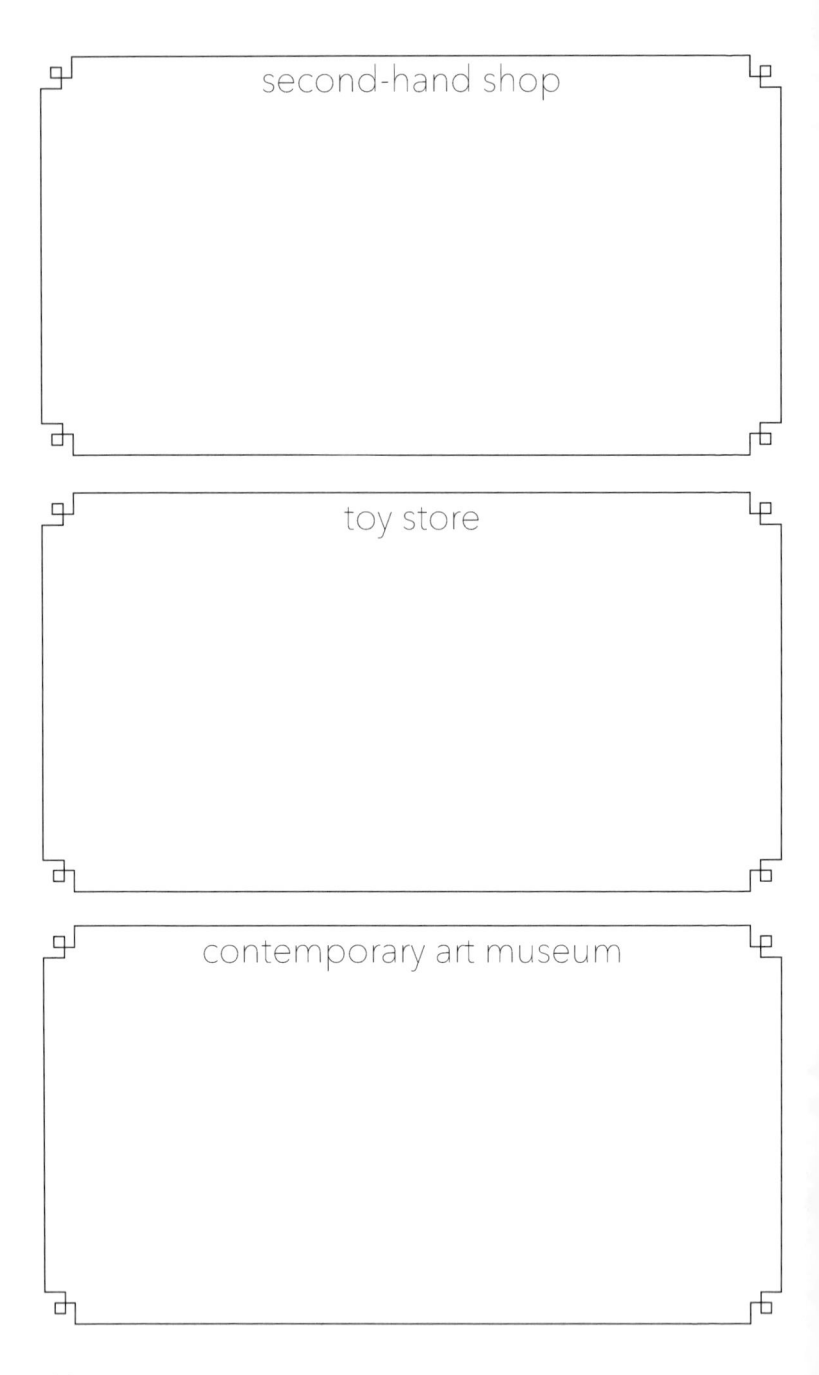

toy store

contemporary art museum

library

friend's house

city street

43

biomimicry inspiration

Find interesting eating behaviors among plants and animals, and maybe even generate ideas inspired by them.

Planet Earth is a wondrous place, and nature provides many sources of inspiration for food designers. The Biomimicry Institute defines biomimicry as "an approach to innovation that seeks sustainable solutions to human challenges by emulating nature's time-tested patterns and strategies." I challenge you to find interesting eating behaviors among plants and animals, and maybe even generate ideas inspired by them.

For example, tobacco trees call for help from nearby predators to fend off the caterpillars of certain hawk moths, leaf bugs, and other pests. Tobacco trees don't just randomly send out a chemical whistle for whatever carnivorous bug happens to be around; they actually call specific predator insects who love to feast on the caterpillars creating the problem in the tree. Whatever is attacking it, it can summon that particular pest's predator. Moreover leafcutter ants are the first animals known to cultivate their own crops like farmers. Their name comes from their ability to cut tree leaves with their scissor-like mandibles. They then each carry a piece of leaf back to the colony where the leaves are added to a pile, similar to a compost heap. Worker ants then add their feces or saliva to the leaves, which acts as a kind of fertilizer to help the leaves grow fungus. They later use the resulting fungus to feed ant larvae. While the baby ants eat the nutrient-rich fungus, adult ants feast on sap that's also produced from the leaves. Quite the example of circular Food Design, right?

Find your own examples of food behavior in other animals and plants, and think of what we can learn from their habits.

looking for inspiration in Nature

plants behaviours

animals behaviours

my Food Design idea using biomimicry

STUDY NATURE, LOVE NATURE, STAY CLOSE TO NATURE. IT WILL NEVER FAIL YOU.

Frank Lloyd Wright

44

free your inner weirdo

activity 1

Part of being a food designer is learning to embrace your inner weirdness, which basically means learning to break away from conformity. Not for everything of course! Waiting in line, stopping at traffic lights, and basic politeness (to mention a few), are wonderful conformities that keep society together. Don't break away from those! But try and recognize and break away from the standard way of looking at things.

Be weird in the way to interpret things and propose insights! Free your creativity from constraints because you know that there is no "wrong" or "less good" idea in Food Design Thinking. So, start breaking that pattern by noticing and focusing on things that others overlook.

Write down everything beautiful and everything improbable about:

beautiful

·····a piece of chewing gum on the ground·····

improbable

beautiful

····· tree bark ·····

improbable

beautiful · the latest spam email you've received · probable

beautiful · a spoon · probable

beautiful ┆ that pair of underwear you never wear ┆ improbable

beautiful ┆ the half-full pack of sugar (or coffee, tea, salt, or baking soda) in your cupboard ┆ improbable

IF AT FIRST THE IDEA IS NOT ABSURD,

Then there is no hope for it.

Albert Einstein

45

free your inner weirdo

activity 2

Laughter puts us at ease, and when we are able to laugh at something we are able to look at it from a fresh perspective. Laughing at what other people might not find laughable is one of the typical behaviors of "weird" people, but it is one of the healthiest behaviors for food designers.

Humor stretches our thinking because creating and laughing at a joke is an exercise in breaking set relationships and links as it forces us to combine ideas that are usually not associated with one another. Combining distant and unrelated ideas is the core of creativity. To become a successful food designer therefore, I suggest you start seeing humor in everything.

By developing the ability to laugh at something, you will develop the ability to see it from multiple perspectives, which is of key importance in Food Design Thinking.

Buy a pizza, make a joke about it, and laugh at it.

Take a frying pan, make a joke about it, and laugh at it.

Take a recipe for tiramisu, make a joke about it, and laugh at it.

Look at a cup of coffee, and concentrate on the empty space in the cup.

What is the essence of that empty space?

Does it need to be filled?

What metaphors does it spark?

46

reverse your viewpoint

Doing things the opposite way, or thinking about certain topics in a way that is contrary to what you would normally do, can be a great way of discovering what you normally overlook. Reversing your perspective is certainly a technique food designers can use to learn to open their thinking.

You, too, can exercise this skill by switching your objective and going in the opposite direction. For example, you can ask yourself: How can I do this less effectively? What would happen if I did this less effectively? By answering these questions your perspective will certainly open up, and more input will influence your projects.

Go to a café of your choice and only consider their rubbish.

Where does it come from?

Where is it going? (will it go)

What can you learn?

Read and follow a recipe from the bottom.

What do you learn about that food-making procedure?

What do you learn about the dish itself?

What do you learn about cooking?

47

get accustomed to random associations

Connecting distant and unrelated ideas is the core essence of creativity. Forcing such correlations, while it might seem daunting, is always quite rewarding. Let's try and do this with the goal of improving or redesigning something. Choose a food that you know very well, a whole dish rather than an ingredient (E.g. spaghetti and meatballs, rather than spaghetti, or fruit salad rather than kiwi, or ramen rather than eggs). Do the following free associations with the goal of redesigning or somehow improving that food. To make it more fun for yourself and more rewarding, make sure that the second object/concept of free association is not at all related to food and eating.

Human beings are very good at finding patterns and associations in the world around them. Thus, whatever word, concept, or object you pick, you will be able to add insights into your problem, develop your idea, or even provide clarification.

Choose a dish that you know very well

Look out the window and write down the third thing you see.

How does it relate to your dish?

How could this be used to redesign or improve your dish?

Open a book, go to page 18, and take the 23rd word.

How does it relate to your dish?

How could this be used to redesign or improve your dish?

Open a browser and Google "word of the day" (dictionary.com is a good website for this). Consider the word you find.

How does it relate to your dish?

How could this be used to redesign or improve your dish?

48

step away from your screen

Creative people need time to do nothing. You too need the time to let your mind wonder. That subconscious wondering generates thoughts that will emerge later on during your conscious creative moments. And sometimes, it is during the subconscious wondering that good, completel ideas bubble up into awareness! So, make sure you allow time to let your mind wonder.

Look outside the window.

Go for a walk.

Pick a flower.

Eat ice cream.

Go to a museum and look at art.

49
wonder

The thing you wonder about should be something nobody else wonders about. Then share your passion with somebody else. The more open you are to sharing your thoughts and invite other thoughts, the more open you'll become to everything.

wonder: *verb* - to be filled with admiration,
    amazement, or awe; to marvel.

Find something wonderful
and wonder at it.

Then, invite other people to
wonder with you.

50

enjoy solitude

We live in a society where there is a lot going on, all the time. Even if we're alone at home, because of our phones, laptops, and Internet connection, there is a lot going on all the time. Technology is fantastic. We all know that, but sometimes it's good to take a break, to switch off. Do that. See what comes out. You can take this break whenever you want, but if you take it in the middle of a creative process, then even better.

Spend one day with no Internet and no electronics. Spend one day with yourself, pen and paper.
Think, write, sketch.

51

write a fan letter

Who is your Food Design hero? Who, in the world of food, design, art, or innovation, is the person you admire the most and whose work inspires you?

Is it a chef, a designer, a writer, a documentary director, an activist, an educator, a researcher, a YouTuber, an engineer, a business owner, or a family member?

Write a fan letter to this person. Write down everything you love about their work and why you love it so much. Write about how they have inspired you and maybe shaped your career. Write about what you take from their work and apply to yours. Print it. Send it.

Yes, do print it (or even better write it by hand), and send it with a nice old stamp. There's nothing better than the nostalgic reading of a tangible letter. And then who knows, you might even get a reply. This is an interesting way to externalize your thoughts, and in doing so, learn about yourself.

52

specifically select random words

Think about the answer
to this question:

What do you love about
food or the act of eating?

then take a magazine or a book, open a random page, and go through the writing. Keep only those words that - in the correct sequence - make a sentence that answers the question above, and cancel all the other words. Sometimes, when forced to answer a question using somebody else's words, we learn more about the topic itself and our thinking around it.

53

take it apart to make it better

A great way to improve something (let's say a product or service that already exists and you want to redesign, or an idea you've had but that you feel is not finished and needs improvement) is to take it apart, and improve each component. Sometimes thinking of improving a product might seem daunting, and we don't know where to start. This technique makes things easier, gives us a structured path to follow, and by making us think about each individual component, allows us to see more and improve more than if we'd consider the whole product or service.

Choose a sandwich (choose a new recipe if you feel adventurous), buy it or make it, eat it. Then buy it or make it again, and this time try and improve each component by asking these questions: Why does this have to be this way? How else can this be accomplished?

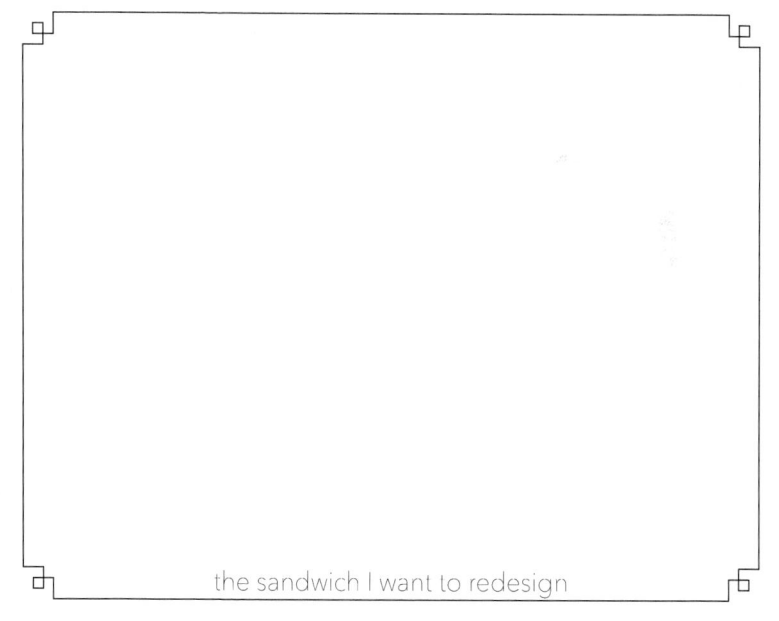

the sandwich I want to redesign

For example, let's take a classic BLT: bacon, lettuce, tomato.

What is the best bread for a BLT?

What ingredients should be in this bread?

What makes each ingredient the best ingredient for this bread?

What is the best texture for a BLT?

Should the bread be cold, warmed up, toasted?

What type of lettuce should it have?

What makes lettuce the best lettuce for BLT?

How should lettuce be cut?

How much lettuce?

What bacon should it use?

How should it be cut and cooked?

How much bacon?

What type of tomato should be used?

How should it be cut?

Should it be seasoned?

With what?

How much tomato?

What other additional ingredient should be added?

What is the best order for the ingredients?

Where should it be added?

etc.

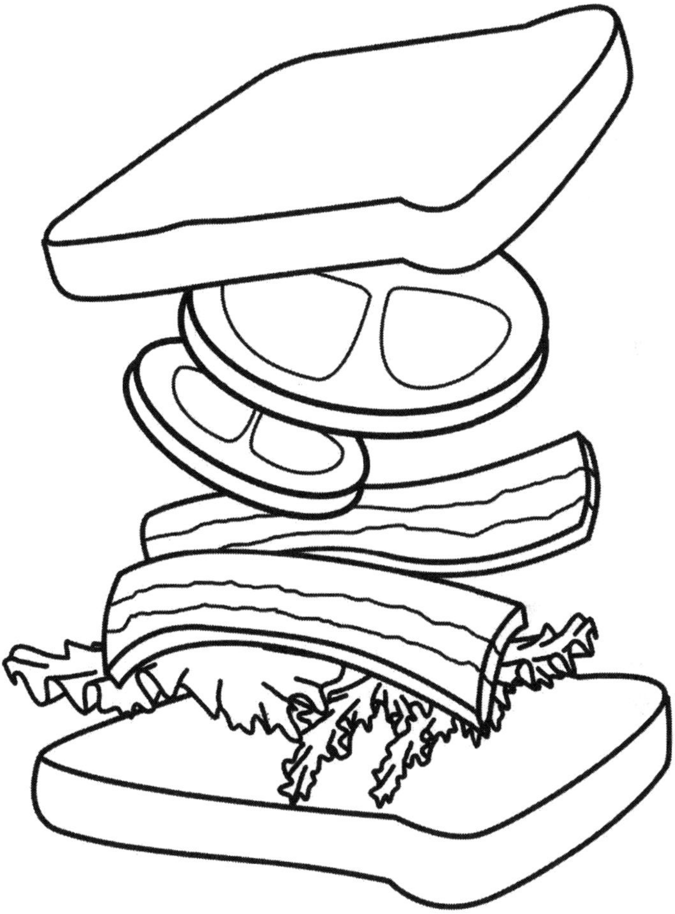

my sandwich
VERSION 2.0

sketch and annotations

what I have added and why

what I have removed and why

what I have changed and why

what I have improved and why

54
substitute

Take elements of your idea and substitute them with something else.

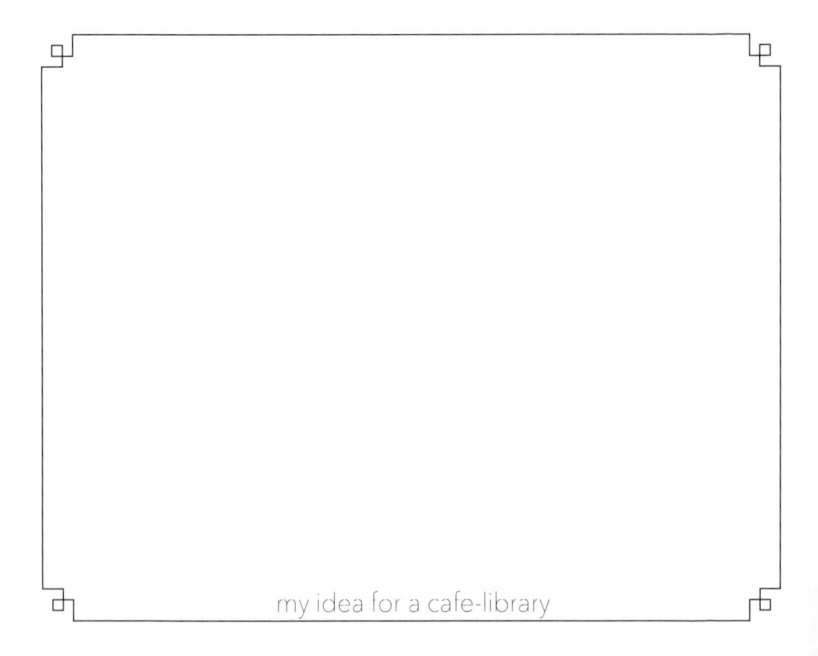

my idea for a cafe-library

Let's train your ability for coming up with ideas. Let's say that you want to come up with an idea for a new cafe-library, one of those places where you sell coffee and give the opportunity to customers to read books there or borrow them. It's a double service: both a coffee shop and a library, because aren't books and coffee great together? (You can choose a design challenge you're already working on, or you can use this example if you're not working on anything at the moment). You have the basic idea; it's now time to make it unique and personal to you. But how? One way is to take elements of your idea and substitute them with something else. You can substitute things, places, procedures, people, ideas, and even emotions. If you're designing a cafe-library because you know that's what you want, maybe you don't need to substitute "coffee" and "library". Instead, try and substitute the most common aspects of a cafe and of a library. Don't be afraid to say something weird! Instead, be as weird as possible. You'll have time later on to go over your ideas and choose what makes more sense. For example: What would happen if you substituted chairs with inflatable sofas? What would happen if you substituted staff members with iPads? What would happen if you substituted relaxation for excitement? What would happen if you substituted biographical books for sci-fi? And so on. For each substitution, write down an idea. In the end - and only in the end! - look at all those ideas and put together those that would make your ideal cafe-library.

substitutions
from 〉 to

my cafe-library
VERSION 2.0

sketch and annotations

55

combine

At the core of creativity is the ability - sometimes the stroke of insight - of combining distant and unrelated ideas. Think about it: the frappuccino was Starbuck's genius idea of combining a cappuccino and a frappé. Johann Gutenberg connected the wine press and the coin punch and invented the printing press with movable type. One day Pablo Picasso found an old bicycle. After looking at it for a while, he removed the handle bars and seat, and he proceeded to weld them together to form the head of a bull.

To train your mind to do the same, here is your task. Combine two of any of the objects in the next page and create a new dish or food product. Once you have an idea, make a sketch of it, and then please… please, please share it with me on my Facebook page! I can't wait to see what you'll come up with!

Combine two objects and create a new idea for a dish or food product.

I combine...

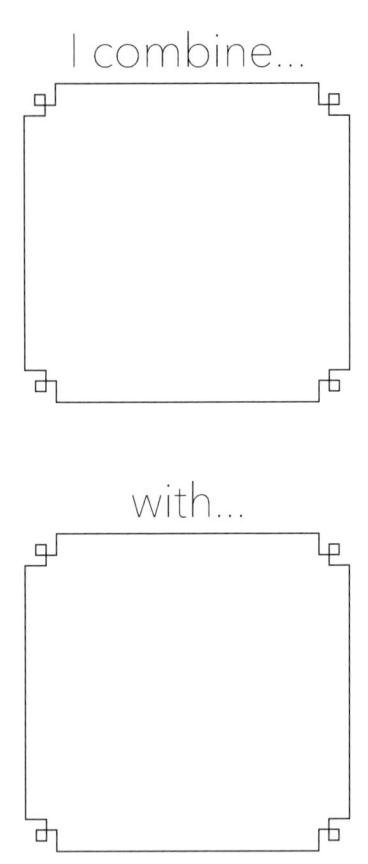

with...

my dish or food product:

sketch and annotations

DISCOVERY CONSISTS OF LOOKING AT THE SAME THING AS EVERYONE ELSE

AND THINKING SOMETHING DIFFERENT

Szent-Györgyi

56

be inspired by others

Make a list of the people who inspire you most. These can be anybody: people you know personally or people you've never met, people who are living or people who have lived before you, people in the Food Design industry or from any other profession. Write down all the things these people have done, designed, thought, or written that truly inspire you and that make you think, "I wish I had done that!" Then, adapt it and make it yours, your object, your project, your idea, your thought, your writing.

Discovering who inspires you and reflecting upon what inspires you is a very good practice for creative people. Food Designers don't always invent the wheel. Most often what they do is adapting somebody else's idea making it into their own proposition. This type of innovation, too, can be radical.

Make a list of the people who inspire you most, and be inspired by their work.

my adaptation						
inspiring thing						
person						

57

make it simple

In the late 1970s, Dieter Rams proposed the 10 principles of good design. The last principle, and my favorite, is: "Good design is as little design as possible." This principle inspires designers - and of course, food designers - to go back to simplicity. Good Food Design should be the excellent design of those aspects that are needed to make the product functional and beautiful, but only of those aspects.

For every object, service, space, or event you see, you can thoroughly analyze it and recognize all the aspects that could be taken out until you are left with the pure essence of what that object/service/space/event should be. If there's nothing else that could be taken out, that's good Food Design.

Choose a food service and simplify it.

Choose one restaurant or cafe of your choice, go there, order something, and sit down. Spend a few minutes, maybe a few hours there, and observe everything. Then make a list of all the things that could be removed. Don't stop at tangible objects like chairs, paintings, and curtains, but reflect on movements, interactions, actions, etc. In the end, make a list of only those aspects that you think are the essence of that place, and should not be removed. Remember the establishment should always aim at being functional as well as aesthetically pleasing.

tangible things to remove

intangible things to remove

what makes the essence of the service

58

senses isolation

What would it be like to experience life with only one sense available? There is much we can learn by simulating our experience of the world with only one of our senses.

Choose a restaurant or cafe near you, go there, order something, and sit down for a while. Focus all your attention on one of your senses only, trying to ignore all the others. Focus only on what you hear, only on what you see, only on what you smell, only on what you taste, or only on what you feel with your skin and sense of touch (remember you don't touch only with your hands, but you touch with the skin in your whole body). Make a map of your sensations. What can you learn about that establishment? What is wonderful? What could be improved? What do you learn about yourself as a food designer?

Experience a restaurant with one sense only.

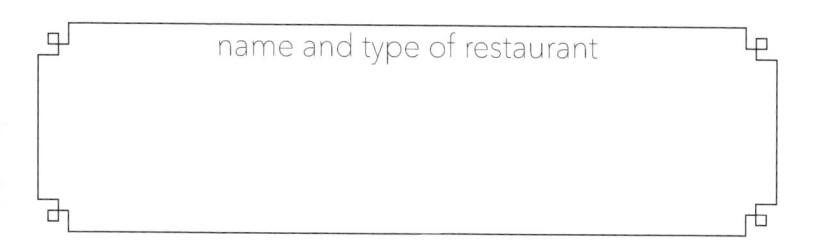

name and type of restaurant

choose one sense:

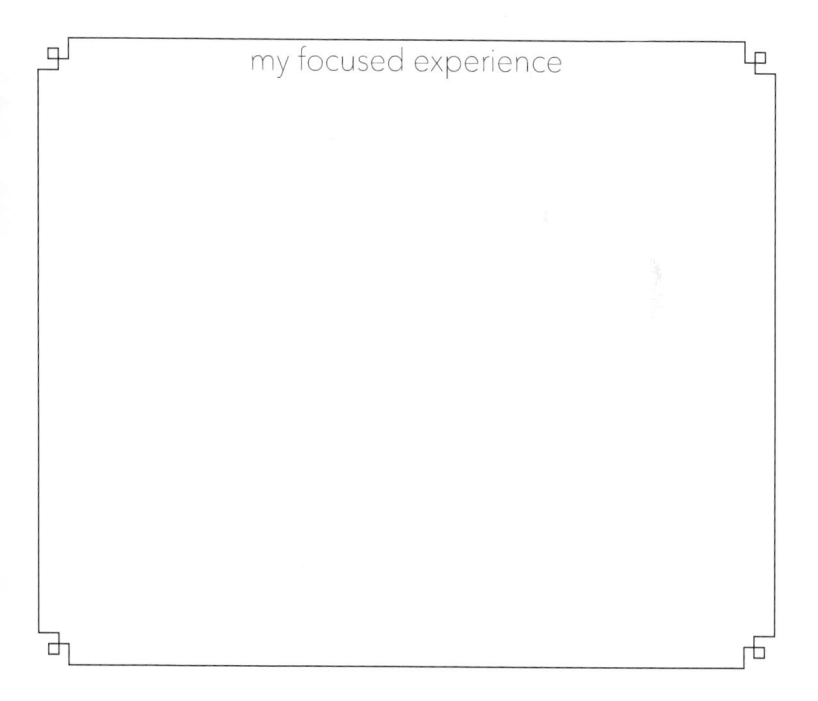

my focused experience

What can you learn about that establishment?

What is wonderful?

What could be improved?

What do you learn about yourself as a food designer?

59

reuse

reuse

reuse

Over the last few decades, too much "one-function designing" has been done. Think of all the objects there are that have one function and one function only. The kitchen seems to be the favorite arena of such products. The banana holder. The five-bladed herb scissors. The strawberry huller (Have you seen it? Please go and Google it, you won't be disappointed…). The cherry pitter. Et cetera. I don't know about you, but it seems to me that these are those products that live their whole life inside a kitchen drawer and maybe see the light once a year. Isn't this a bit of a waste of resources? So I challenge you to go to your kitchen (or your mum's kitchen, your friend's kitchen, your neighbor's kitchen), find one of these one-function objects (as I like to call them) that you never use, and design a second use for it. The challenge is to not redesign the object, or any aspect of it, but only find a second use for it. When you do, please share it with me on my Facebook page because I'm so curious to see what you'll think about!

Go to your kitchen, find a one-function object, and design a second use for it.

my one-function object

its first function:

its second function:

60

what's next for this waste?

Go to your kitchen rubbish bin right now, and look inside. If you live in a town where you're required to recycle then look inside all your bins. What do you see? Let me tell you what you see… TOO MUCH STUFF! Think about the amount of stuff we throw away every day. Most of it comes from our kitchen, and it's a consequence of us cooking and eating. We must eat because it is a necessity, and as a consequence we produce a lot of rubbish. This is a humongous waste of resources, in terms of the energy, materials, and human effort that has gone into making and distributing that packaging and that will go into disposing of it. Not to mention their impact on the environment. Now, while you're there with your head over your rubbish bin, how do you feel? Sad? Disheartened? That's okay, because what I'd like you to do now is shift your attention on the fact that you're a food designer! You are an innovator and a change maker. You have been put on this planet to inspire others. Let's start from your own rubbish bin.

Take at least one item from your rubbish bin and find a way to use it, to extend its life beyond what it was originally designed to do.

Then take a picture and share it with your friends and family.

You can start changing the world with something as simple as making a simple change, and inspiring others to do the same. You can start changing the world right now.

BE THE CHANGE THAT YOU WISH TO SEE IN THE WORLD

Mahatma Gandhi

pat yourself on the back!

You made it! You've dived into two months of mind-training exercises, and you've emerged a better food designer. I am very proud of you =).

Now you have the skills, the mindset, and the right attitude to develop any Food Design project, whether it's designing a new dish, a kitchen appliance, a food event, or your own Food Design career. The skills and the mindset you've developed will be priceless in your use of Food Design Thinking or any other way you'll venture into food creativity.

Now go out there and make things happen. I know I will love to see what you accomplish within the fabulous world that is Food Design.

Happy Food Design!

Francesca

notes

WHO DO I KNOW?

Teachers, Web Devs, Non-Profits, Biomeds, Queers, Deafs, Women, Postal, Deppressed, Cooks, Hospital, Elderly

WHO IS LEFT BEHIND?
POC, WOMEN, QUEERS, Deafs, Crips, Elderly, Homeless ESL, Refugees, Relig Minorities

*FOSTER SYSTEM / CHILD HOMELESSNESS / YOUTH IN CARE

What is THROWN AWAY?
Styrofoam, mixed packaging, Soft plastics, plastic bags. cups - coffee

WHAT'S BEING HACKED?
clear masks, homeless shelters, diabetic covers, cut clothes

WHO AM I?
Queer, sex pos, repro health, sustainable inclusive, Deaf,

notes

notes

notes

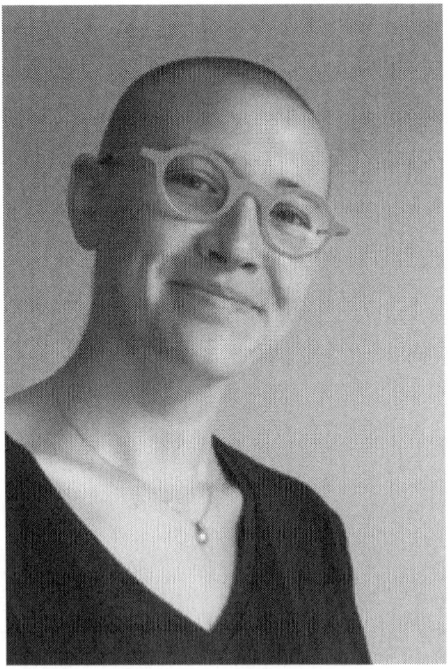

about the author

Dr. Francesca Zampollo is a Food Design researcher, consultant, keen public speaker, teacher, HuffingtonPost writer, and YouTuber. She is the founder of the Online School of Food Design© (the first and only provider of online education on Food Design). Francesca has a PhD in Design Theory applied to Food Design and is an award winning Food Designer. She is currently developing and theorizing further Food Design Thinking, a branch of Design Thinking she has proposed in 2012. She is the founding editor of the International Journal of Food Design, and in 2009 she founded the International Food Design Society. Francesca has organized the first, second, and third International Conference on Food Design, and taught Design Theory and Food Design at London Metropolitan University and Auckland University of Technology as a senior lecturer.

Manufactured by Amazon.ca
Bolton, ON